C. 1

LANGUAGE ARTS EXPLORER

U.S. GROWTH AND CHANGE IN THE 19th CENTURY

1801 to 1861

by Brian Howell

HISTORY DIGS

CHERRY LAKE PUBLISHING • ANN ARBOR, MICHIGAN

CHERRY LAKE Publishing

Published in the United States of America
by Cherry Lake Publishing
Ann Arbor, Michigan
www.cherrylakepublishing.com

Printed in the United States of America
Corporate Graphics Inc
September 2011
CLFA09

Consultants: Brett Barker, associate professor of history, University of Wisconsin–Marathon County; Gail Saunders–Smith, associate professor of literacy, Beeghly College of Education, Youngstown State University

Editorial direction:
Rebecca Rowell

Design and production:
Marie Tupy

Photo credits: North Wind Picture Archives, cover, 1, 5, 7, 9, 10, 13, 16, 19, 21, 22, 23; Tischenko Irina/Shutterstock Images, 8; Christophe Testi/Shutterstock Images, 11; Shutterstock Images, 14; Jerry Moorman/iStockphoto, 15; H. B. Lindsley/Library of Congress, 25; Sue Smith/Shutterstock Images, 27; iStockphoto, 30

Library of Congress Cataloging-in-Publication Data
Howell, Brian, 1974-
 US growth and change in the 19th century / by Brian Howell.
     p. cm. – (Language arts explorer–History digs)
  ISBN 978-1-61080-202-4 – ISBN 978-1-61080-290-1 (pbk.)
  1. United States–History–19th century–Juvenile literature. 2. United States–Territorial expansion–History–19th century–Juvenile literature. 3. Industrial revolution–United States--Juvenile literature. 4. California–Gold discoveries–Juvenile literature. 5. Slavery–Southern States–History–19th century–Juvenile literature. I. Title. II. Title: U.S. growth and change in the 19th century.
 E337.5.H68 2011
 973.5–dc22
                                                                2011015127

Cherry Lake Publishing would like to acknowledge the work of The Partnership for 21st Century Skills. Please visit www.21stCenturySkills.org for more information.

TABLE OF CONTENTS

You are being given a mission. The facts in What You Know will help you accomplish it. Remember the clues from What You Know while you are reading the story. The clues and the story will help you answer the questions at the end of the book. Have fun on this adventure!

YOUR MISSION

Your mission is to learn to think like a historian. What tools do historians use to research the past? What kinds of questions do they ask, and where do they look for answers? On this assignment, your goal is to learn about expansion and reform in the United States during the nineteenth century. How did the United States expand its territory? Who were Lewis and Clark? How did railroad technology help the United States in its expansion? What made people travel to California? How did expansion affect American Indians? How did Americans respond to slavery? As you learn, remember What You Know.

WHAT YOU KNOW

★ American Indians lived in all of what is now the contiguous United States before European settlers arrived.

★ In 1800, the Mississippi River was the western border of the United States. Most of what we know as the United States today was owned by Spain, France, and Russia.

★ Settlers moved and populated the West during the 1800s.

★ By 1867, the United States had grown to include all of the land that is the contiguous United States.

★ Slavery was part of the culture and economy in the southern United States.

Artifacts such as the diary William Clark kept while exploring the West are valuable resources to historians.

Use this book to explore history in ways a historian might. A student is exploring U.S. history during this time while on a school field trip to a local museum. The student kept a journal. Read the journal to carry out your mission.

Today, my class took a field trip to a museum. We spent the whole day learning about U.S. history in the 1800s. When we arrived at the museum, we met our tour guide, Mr. Patrick. He told us we would get to study many artifacts. Our first stop was to see a copy of the Louisiana Purchase **Treaty**.

A Lot of Land for Little Money

"The Louisiana Purchase," Mr. Patrick said, "was the biggest purchase of land in U.S. history."

He explained that before the Louisiana Purchase was made in 1803, there were only 17 U.S. states. With an area of 885,000 square miles, the Louisiana Purchase more than doubled the size of the United States. There was a map of the purchase next to the treaty that showed what the United States got when it bought the Louisiana Territory from France. The territory included much more than Louisiana. It included land that became all or part of Louisiana, Arkansas, Missouri, Iowa, Minnesota, Texas, Oklahoma, Kansas, Nebraska, South Dakota, North Dakota, New Mexico, Colorado, Wyoming, and Montana.

"Why would France give up that much land?" I asked.

"France's leader," explained Mr. Patrick, "was Napoléon I, or Napoléon Bonaparte. He had hopes of creating a French empire in the West that included using Louisiana. But things did not work out the way he had planned. Louisiana would be a great source of grains and other supplies to feed the French slaves in the Caribbean. France had established a **colony** in Saint-Domingue (now Haiti), but had lost control of it. Disease was also a problem. More than 40,000 soldiers

This map of the Louisiana Purchase shows how it more than doubled the size of the United States.

died fighting to regain control of the colony. Others had been affected by yellow fever."

"Napoléon I must not have had much of an army left," I said.

"Well, he had some troops, and around this time, problems with Great Britain arose. So, France needed its troops to fight the British. That left France unable to defend the French territory in the West. Napoléon I also needed money to fund the new war in Europe, so he decided to sell the territory."

"Wow, France had a lot going on. But it turned out to be a good thing for the United States," I chimed in.

"That's right, it was," he agreed.

I learned that Thomas Jefferson, who was president at the time, wanted to purchase New Orleans from France. Robert R. Livingston and James Monroe, two U.S. government officials, were authorized to pay as much as $10 million for New Orleans. Instead, France offered the United States a chance to buy all of the Louisiana Territory for $15 million. Livingston and Monroe quickly took the deal.

I asked what the United States wanted to do with all of that land. To answer that question, Mr. Patrick took us to another **exhibit**. It was about the explorers Meriwether Lewis and William Clark.

Lewis and Clark

"Even before the Louisiana Purchase, Jefferson wanted to find out what was out west," Mr. Patrick said. "He wanted to know if there was a direct water route across the continent. Finding one might cut down travel time between the coasts. The Louisiana Purchase opened the door for Lewis and Clark to begin exploring that area of the continent."

I explored the exhibit. I read that the Lewis and Clark **expedition** began in May 1804 with a team of 33 people and finished in September 1806.

I studied a map of the journey. It began in St. Louis, Missouri. The explorers traveled north along the Missouri River. That took them into the area that is now the Dakotas. From there, the expedition headed west into what is now Montana, Idaho, Washington, and Oregon.

The exhibit included replicas of many artifacts from the Lewis and Clark expedition,

Maps can be very helpful in understanding a topic.
This one shows that Lewis and Clark's expedition was really long.

including journals written by the explorers. The men sketched fish, birds, and plants they had discovered. There were other items as well, such as compasses, a telescope, tools, medical instruments, and a shaving kit. American Indian artifacts were also in the exhibit. I saw pipes, clothing, and tools.

As I studied these items, I learned that Lewis and Clark had many encounters—some friendly, some not—with American Indian tribes. In one, Lewis and Clark met Sacagawea, a woman from the Shoshone tribe. She went with them on their expedition. She helped them talk and trade with other tribes. She was the only woman on the journey and proved to be a valuable member of the group. Mr. Patrick told us Sacagawea had a baby boy, Jean-Baptiste Charbonneau, on February 11, 1805.

"Because Lewis and Clark had Sacagawea and the baby with them," Mr. Patrick said, "American Indian tribes felt the group was friendly. That made future encounters with American Indians much more peaceful."

Lewis and Clark learned there is not a direct water route across the continent. Though they did not confirm what the president had hoped, their discoveries were invaluable for the United States. ★

LASTING LEGACY

Lewis and Clark were the first white men to record descriptions of many animals, including the prairie dog and grizzly bear. Lewis discovered and named a type of woodpecker: Lewis's Woodpecker. Clark discovered and named another bird: Clark's Nutcracker. Lewis and Clark's maps helped the United States learn about the territory west of the Mississippi River. Some of the names Lewis and Clark gave to their discoveries are still intact, including Great Falls on the Missouri River in Montana.

After looking at the Lewis and Clark exhibit, Mr. Patrick took us to another part of the museum. As we walked, I thought about how Lewis and Clark's journey took two and a half years. I realized how fast we get from one place to the next today—even to other countries. I wondered how people could travel so far in the 1800s when it took so long. Just then, we got to our next stop at the museum. It was all about trains.

Mapping the Routes

Mr. Patrick explained that there were few railways in the United States at the time of Lewis and Clark. As the country grew, so did the desire for faster travel. In the 1800s, the construction of railroads was one of the great additions to the United States.

In the museum, there was a life-size train engine on display. It was really big. But what caught my attention were the maps on the walls that showed some of the nation's early railroad lines. One map was a replica of a map made in 1828 by James Hayward. It was a proposed Boston and Providence Railway and is the earliest known **topographic** map that shows a railroad **survey**.

"What's a railroad survey?" I asked.

Mr. Patrick explained, "To make a map, mapmakers had to learn the land, a practice called surveying. Explorers such as Lewis and Clark helped survey the land. Surveying showed railroad engineers where mountains and bodies of water were located. Places with good, solid ground also were identified. That's where engineers wanted the tracks to be laid."

"So, surveying was really important to building railroads?" I asked.

"Yes, because routes had to be planned before track could be laid," he answered. "Once the land was surveyed, maps were made. Maps were once engraved on copper plates, which took time and made mapmaking a much slower process than it is now. But advances in printing technology in the early 1800s meant maps could be produced faster."

"And that helped make building railroads faster," I jumped in.

"Exactly," Mr. Patrick confirmed.

Railroading Begins

Continuing through the exhibit, I saw a map of the Baltimore and Ohio Railroad. I learned the railroad, known as the B&O for short, launched **railroading** in the United States in 1827. It was the first long-distance commercial railroad track and the first passenger carrier. The line wasn't very big when it started. It was 14 miles long in 1830, but it grew to approximately 500 miles by the time of the Civil War in the early 1860s.

During the next couple of decades, there were a lot of railroads built around the United States. From 1863 to 1869, workers laid 1,776 miles of track to complete the transcontinental railroad. It stretched from Omaha, Nebraska, to Sacramento, California. The transcontinental railroad connected to existing railroads, uniting the East with areas west of the Mississippi River. Its growth aided expansion, prompting people to move westward and towns to form—some seemed to spring up almost overnight. The railroad opened new, growing markets for manufactured goods and steel.

Advertisements are useful in understanding a culture or a period.
This one shows that the railroad was growing
and invited people to enjoy the new and exciting technology.

CONNECTING THE COUNTRY

The invention of railroads in the 1800s allowed people to travel long distances faster than ever. The trip that took Lewis and Clark more than two years to complete took only nine days by rail—round-trip! The railroad also transported resources and goods more easily. By 1861, there were more than 31,000 miles of track in the United States. The peak came in 1916, when there were more than 270,000 miles of track. In 2009, there were still more than 160,000 miles of track.

This helped fuel the Industrial Revolution, which dramatically changed much of the wild frontier Lewis and Clark had discovered in the West in the early 1800s.

Trains always seemed like just something fun to ride. I learned how important they have been to the United States. ★

After leaving the railroad exhibit, I thought about everything we had learned so far. I was curious to know what made people want to move to the West.

"In the 1800s, there were a lot of changes that made getting to the West easier," I said. "But why would people go somewhere that wasn't really developed?"

Mr. Patrick answered, "People in the East were attracted to the West because there were great opportunities to own land and to have a better living."

John Sutter

One person who decided to move west was John Sutter. Born Johann August Suter, the German-born Swiss man immigrated to the United States in search of a better life. Sutter settled in California and became part of U.S. history as a pioneer in the California gold rush.

The next exhibit we visited at the museum was about the California gold rush of the 1840s. Mr. Patrick told us that gold was first discovered on Sutter's land in California. The exhibit had a lot of cool things in it, including tools used to **pan** for gold and maps.

My favorite part of the exhibit was Sutter's diary. There was a copy of it and an article Sutter wrote in 1857 that was published in *Hutchings' California Magazine*. The article was Sutter's account of the gold discovery.

John Sutter's pioneering spirit had lasting effects on California. This portrait and Sutter's own diary help us to better understand him and what life was like in California during the gold rush.

"Sutter left Missouri in 1838," Mr. Patrick told us. "In California, Sutter wrote in his diary about building a fort and contending with American Indians in the area."

Mr. Patrick said Sutter's Fort was located in what is now Sacramento, the capital of California. Sutter wrote in 1844:

> *The fort was built in about 4 years of time, as it was very difficult to get the necessary lumber we was sawing by hand Oak timber*

Sutter also wrote about **immigrants** often coming through his area. He let a lot of them stay at his fort. He also put many of them to work. Sutter hired people to build a flour **mill** and a sawmill. One of the men he hired was James W. Marshall. In August 1847, Sutter noted in his diary that Marshall "began to work briskly on the sawmill."

Discovering Gold

On January 28, 1848, Sutter wrote about Marshall again. He had come to Sutter's home to discuss something important.

> *He showed me the first Specimens of Gold, that is he was not certain if it was Gold or not, but he thought it might be; immediately I made the proof and found that it was Gold.*

Marshall had discovered the gold while working on the sawmill for Sutter. It was the first discovery of gold in the California Territory. Sutter asked his employees to keep the discovery a secret for six weeks while his flour mill was being finished. But they didn't honor his request. Word of the gold discovery spread quickly. Thousands of people went to the West in search of gold over the next several years.

"What happened to Sutter? Did he get a lot of business from the settlers?" I asked.

"No, just the opposite," Mr. Patrick responded. "The discovery of gold ruined his business plans. His workers joined the search for gold. Without employees, he lost income. And gold seekers stole from him. Here, read Sutter's last diary entry."

I looked where Mr. Patrick pointed and read aloud, "Without having discovered the Gold, I would have become the richest wealthiest man on the Pacific Shore." I was amazed how one small thing could make such a difference. Sutter's plans were ruined, but California was changed forever. ★

GOING TO CALIFORNIA

The California population in 1860 was four times what it was in 1850 because of gold. In 1852 alone, 20,000 people arrived. Several thousand Chinese moved to California during that time, and their work building the transcontinental railroad in the 1860s was invaluable. There was a period during construction when 80 percent of laborers for one railroad line—8,000 of 10,000—were Chinese. Their work, including handling dangerous explosives, helped advance the railroad and the nation.

The discovery of gold at Sutter's sawmill quickly turned into a gold rush.
This is one artist's depiction of the event.

After seeing the California gold rush exhibit, I couldn't stop thinking about the American Indians who lived in the 1800s. I wondered what happened to all of them during this time of great expansion. Fortunately, Mr. Patrick took us to an exhibit about American Indians.

I had learned in school that many tribes were in the United States long before Europeans began settling here—long before the United States was a nation. When we got to the exhibit, we learned about the fate of those people as a result of expansion.

Losing Their Land

"One of the most well-known American Indian tribes is the Cherokee," Mr. Patrick explained. "The ancestors of the Cherokee— and the Choctaw, another tribe—had been living in southeastern North America for thousands of years."

We studied some Cherokee and Choctaw artifacts as Mr. Patrick spoke. I saw an arrowhead, a bowl, and a basket. There were weapons, including an ax and a bow and arrow. There were furs that were used for warmth during winter.

I noticed a document on the wall. "Andrew Jackson, President of the United States of America." was written across the top.

Mr. Patrick told us, "When Jackson was president, he signed the Indian Removal Act into law in 1830. The document on the wall is a replica of what Jackson signed. He and others wanted Indian lands, so they forced them to leave. He wanted to move the Indians west to make way for white **settlements**."

As the United States expanded, railroads and settlers intruded on lands that American Indians had lived on for a very long time.

The Indian Removal Act offered tribes land in the West if they would give up their land in the East. Some of the tribes took the offer and moved. Others stayed and became citizens of the states in which they lived. Still others were forced by the U.S. government to leave.

Roughly 100,000 American Indians were removed from the East in the 1830s, including 15,000 to 21,500 Cherokees. As the Cherokee and other tribes were forced west, thousands of them died during their move. At least 4,000 Cherokee died.

OKLAHOMA

Many American Indian tribes settled on reservations in the area that is now Oklahoma. Several tribes were already in the territory at the time. The Cherokee and Choctaw, who were forced to leave the southeast, occupied two of the largest chunks of land, in eastern Oklahoma. The territory was home to many other tribes, including the Creek, Cheyenne, Chickasaw, Arapahoe, Iowa, and Pawnee. Many cities in Oklahoma are named after tribes. The name Oklahoma comes from a Choctaw word that means "red people," which was a term often used to describe American Indians.

"The journey became known as the Trail of Tears, and the route has since become a national landmark," Mr. Patrick said. "The trail runs through nine states: Alabama, Arkansas, Georgia, Illinois, Kentucky, Missouri, North Carolina, Oklahoma, and Tennessee."

As I examined more of the exhibit, I learned that many American Indians who survived were introduced to U.S. government and culture and adopted many white traditions.

"But where did they live?" I asked. "With all the settlers in the West, was there somewhere for the American Indians to go?"

"In the end," Mr. Patrick said, "they were given new lands in the West that were designated solely for American Indians. The United States took over approximately 25 million acres of land from the American Indians in the East. That allowed for white settlements and the spread of slavery." ★

After learning about the experiences of American Indians, my class made its last stop in the museum. The final exhibit was about slavery. We learned in history class that slavery existed in some states long ago.

Slavery

"Slavery is when people hold other people against their will and force them to work," Mr. Patrick said. "The enslaved people are treated as property, not as equals. This was an issue that caused many problems throughout the country and even divided the United States."

The practice of slavery was used in the United States from the time it was a collection of colonies. It existed in the southern states. Many people in the northern states thought slavery was wrong, however. Eventually, the issue of slavery erupted as part of the Civil War, which lasted from 1861 to 1865. By that time, there were almost 4 million slaves in the South.

Harriet Tubman

As we were walking through this exhibit, Mr. Patrick told us more about slavery. While he was talking, I noticed a photograph on the wall of an African American woman. I asked who she was.

"That is Harriet Tubman," Mr. Patrick said. "She helped free more than 300 slaves."

"All by herself? How did she do that?" I asked.

"By the Underground Railroad," he answered.

Mr. Patrick described the Underground Railroad. He taught us that it wasn't really underground or a railroad. It was a secret system in which people helped slaves escape to the free northern states or to Canada. The slaves who escaped were considered the passengers on the Underground Railroad. Tubman was a conductor. She helped the slaves by directing them to freedom.

"Tubman was a slave who escaped," he said. "After escaping, she made 19 trips back to the South to help other slaves become free. On her first few trips, she helped her family members to freedom. After that, she helped as many others as possible."

"Since she had escaped, and slavery was still legal in the South, that must have been dangerous to keep going back," I said.

"Yes, it was very dangerous," he confirmed. "Tubman and other conductors had to be careful not to get caught. They had to be smart and clever to help the passenger slaves get to the North. They traveled at night and would often hide in barns. Tubman's efforts became so well known that Southerners offered a $40,000 **reward** for her capture."

ADJUSTING TO FREEDOM

Escaping the South and earning freedom was only part of the journey for the slaves who traveled the Underground Railroad. After finding their freedom, the former slaves had to learn how to live on their own. Through the help of others, they settled onto new land and into homes of their own. They also had to get jobs and learn to provide for themselves.

Harriet Tubman's brave work as part of the Underground Railroad changed the lives of countless Americans—conductors and passengers alike.

"I hope she wasn't captured," I whispered.

"No, Tubman was never caught," Mr. Patrick said. "And she never lost a passenger. With the help of Tubman and other conductors, including John Fairfield and Levi Coffin, thousands of slaves escaped the South for freedom in the North. Still, those who escaped made up only a small fraction of the number of people enslaved."

Learning about the Underground Railroad was amazing. Escaping to the North was not easy. The passengers often traveled hundreds of miles. But with the help of people along the way, including friendly white people who sometimes provided food and shelter, the Underground Railroad was the path to freedom.

I have learned so much about the expansion and growth of the United States during this field trip. I didn't realize how much important information is so close to home. I will definitely visit the museum again. ★

MISSION ACCOMPLISHED!

You did it! You have learned about expansion and reform in the United States during the nineteenth century. You discovered that the United States more than doubled in size with the Louisiana Purchase. You now know that Lewis and Clark helped the United States learn about the territory west of the Mississippi River. You found out that railroad technology connected the coasts and brought great change to the country. Also, you learned that American Indian tribes were forced from their lands onto reservations and that thousands of slaves found freedom using the Underground Railroad. Good job!

CONSIDER THIS

★ Lewis and Clark discovered many animals, plants, and landmarks. What are some of the unique plants and animals in your home state?

★ Think about the thousands of people who headed to California during the gold rush. Would you be willing to move to a place you had never seen before to pursue a dream?

★ Why would some people support slavery?

★ There were many slaves who risked their lives in search of freedom. What does freedom mean to you?

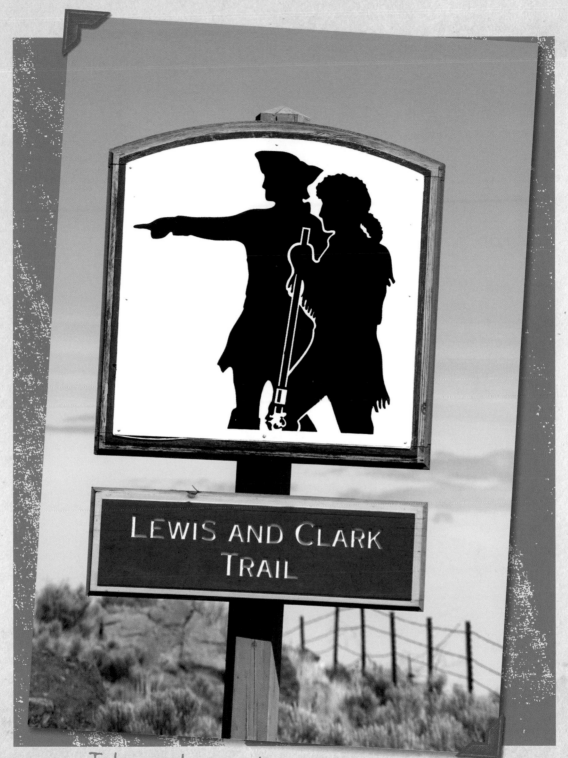

Today, people can explore the United States
using the same route Lewis and Clark took on their expedition.

GLOSSARY

artifact (ART-uh-fakt) an object made by people in the past

colony (KAH-luh-nee) a territory belonging to and ruled by a distant nation

exhibit (ig-ZIB-it) a collection of objects placed in a public area for people to see

expedition (ek-spuh-DISH-uhn) a trip taken to explore an area

immigrant (IM-i-gruhnt) a person who settles in one country after leaving another

mill (mil) a building with machinery used for a specific purpose, such as sawing wood or grinding grain into flour

pan (pan) to look for gold by washing gravel or sand in a pan or a sieve

railroading (RAYL-roh-ding) the building or running of a railroad

reservation (rez-ur-VAY-shuhn) land set aside by the government to be used for something specific, such as a home for a tribe of American Indians

reward (ri-WORD) money given for finding someone or something

settlement (SET-uhl-muhnt) a small community of people

survey (sur-VAY) to examine and measure land to learn its condition and character and to make a map

topographic (TAHP-ah-graf-ik) having to do with the details of a landscape, including its hills, valleys, lakes, and rivers

treaty (TREE-tee) a formal agreement between two parties, generally in reference to peace or land

LEARN MORE

BOOKS

Fradin, Dennis Brindell. *The California Gold Rush*. Tarrytown, NY: Marshall Cavendish Benchmark, 2008.

Sawyer, Kem Knapp. *Harriet Tubman*. New York, NY: DK, 2010.

Schaffer, David. *The Louisiana Purchase: The Deal of the Century that Doubled the Nation*. Berkeley Heights, NJ: Enslow, 2006.

Schanzer, Rosalyn. *How We Crossed The West: The Adventures of Lewis & Clark*. Des Moines, IA: National Geographic Society, 2002.

WEB SITES

Lewis & Clark
http://www.nationalgeographic.com/lewisandclark/

This National Geographic site includes an interactive journey log, a timeline, and a list of the discoveries Lewis and Clark made on their expedition.

National Museum of the American Indian
http://www.nmai.si.edu/

Explore the many tribes of North, Central, and South America.

Slavery and the Making of America
http://www.pbs.org/wnet/slavery/

Learn about slavery through firsthand accounts at this PBS site.

MISSION 1

Meriwether Lewis and William Clark explored the West and discovered a lot of new animals and plants. Research some of their discoveries. Are any of the plants and animals now extinct? Do they still exist where the explorers discovered them? Do any of them live in areas beyond where Lewis and Clark discovered them? Find out more about the animals and plants that live in your state. What is your state animal? What is your state bird? What is your state flower or tree? Do any of these things live or grow in your neighborhood? Explore your neighborhood and record what you see and who you meet.

MISSION 2

In the 1800s, many people moved to the West in search of gold. Today, people still pan for gold. Find out if there are places in your area where you can learn to pan for gold. What methods and techniques are used today to pan for gold? In what areas of the United States is gold panning most popular?

INDEX

ABOUT THE AUTHOR

Brian Howell is a freelancer who writes about sports and history. He has a bachelor's degree in journalism, with a minor in history. He lives with his wife and four children in his native Colorado.

ABOUT THE CONSULTANTS

Brett Barker is an associate professor of history at the University of Wisconsin-Marathon County in Wausau. He received his PhD in history from the University of Wisconsin-Madison and his MA and BA in history from Ohio State University. He has worked with K-12 teachers in two Teaching American History grants.

Gail Saunders-Smith is a former classroom teacher and Reading Recovery teacher leader. Currently, she teaches literacy courses at Youngstown State University in Ohio. Gail is the author of many books for children and three professional books for teachers.